THE CANCER DIARIES

A Story of Wonder, Darkness and Hope

by

Byron Leavitt

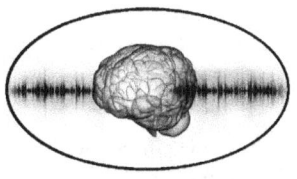

Brain Waves Press

The Cancer Diaries. Copyright © 2014 by Byron Leavitt. All rights reserved.

This book may be reproduced, in whole or in part, provided all excerpts are properly attributed to the author.

Feel free to share this book. Quote away to your heart's content. However, if you do, would you mind dropping me a line to let me know? You can reach me at byron@byronleavitt.com.

Unless otherwise noted, images are copyright © 2014 by Can Stock Photo. You can reach them at http://www.canstockphoto.com.

Except for the Cancer Journal pictures. (Obviously.)

Cover art by Byron Leavitt/Can Stock Photo.

Cover and interior design by Byron Leavitt.

Unless otherwise noted, all Scripture quotations are from The ESV® Bible (The Holy Bible, English Standard Version®), copyright © 2001 by Crossway, a publishing ministry of Good News Publishers. Used by permission. All rights reserved.

Most of this content was originally published on my blog "Life Springs" at http://www.lifespringseternal.com. If you enjoy this book, go there and sign up for my email list to get more like it every week!

Inquiries can be addressed to:

Byron Leavitt
byron@byronleavitt.com
(253) 310-6631

Seriously, I'd love to hear from you!

First edition September 2014.

Published by Brain Waves Press. Learn more about Brain Waves at http://www.brainwavespress.com.

ISBN-13: 978-0-9907235-0-9 (Printed Book)
ISBN-13: 978-0-9907235-1-6 (eBook)
ISBN-13: 978-0-9907235-2-3 (Audio Book)

Table of Contents

Hello.	1
The Cancer Journal Part 1	3
Wondering and Grateful	7
The Cancer Journal Part 2	10
Dare to Hope	15
Beauty in the Rain	19
Coauthoring Our Destinies	22
The Cancer Journal Part 3	26
There is Peace	32
Cross-Stitched Lives	35
This Island, Man	39
The Cancer Journal Part 4	43
Our Healer	48
Life Springs Eternal	53
Where We Go From Here	58
Until Next Time.	63
About Byron	66
Want More Wonder?	67
What Did You Think?	67
References	68
Acknowledgments	71

For my girls and my God, who always bring me through.

Hello.
(An Introduction)

It was in late 2013 that I became deeply, oppressively sick. When I reached the point where I could no longer function we went to the emergency room and spent the day before Christmas Eve undergoing a battery of tests. These tests led to a diagnosis some weeks later of stage four Hodgkin's Lymphoma.

I went into treatment, and four months later the cancer was incredibly, miraculously gone. But that's not where the journey ended.

In a nutshell that's the gist of this little book. But you will find it's also about peace, hope, courage, suffering, darkness and light, to name a few. It's about never giving up. It's about free will and destiny. And it's about wonder. Wonder at the world we live in, and wonder at the God whose fingerprints we see stamped all over our everyday lives.

As I started down this road of brokenness and restoration I started writing. I posted these random thoughts online, and people seemed to identify with them. It is many of these writings that are collected here for you.

They are roughly halfway in chronological order and half not. For example, throughout the pages that follow you will see pieces of "The Cancer Journal". "The Cancer Journal" was originally written one piece after the other near the end of this sequence, but it made sense to me to intersperse it throughout this book. Maybe you'll agree. As much as possible, though, I tried to keep things as close to the timeline as I could, so you could see what I was thinking as life moved on.

After all, this is more than just a little bundle of tiny ponderings. This is a story. My story, in fact. But I hope that, as we journey on, you will find that it is your story, too. During our lives we will all venture into the darkness and the storm. Maybe you're there already. The question, however, isn't if we're going in: the question is, will we find the light to guide us through once we're there?

May this story shine that light for you. May it strengthen you in the dark days. And in the end, when the last page is flipped, may it make you wonder.

    Your Friend,

    Byron Leavitt

The Cancer Journal
Part One

I don't know exactly when the itching began. I do know, however, that it started inconspicuously as some mild irritation on my calves. My wife, Sarah, thought it was an allergic reaction to body wash, so we started cycling through all sorts of different soaps to get rid of it. Strangely, nothing seemed to work. The symptoms were pretty tame and thus largely ignored for quite some time. How long I can't say: six months? A year?

In any case, the problem slowly, implacably escalated until the fall of 2013 when I finally admitted the itching was no longer "pretty tame." It spread off my calves to other parts of my body, and with each passing week grew more intense. I continued to live with it, trying to find other solutions, and slowly I became more and more miserable. In late October or early November the itching had consumed my entire body. I had hundreds of bloody open wounds ranging across just about every inch of my skin. Sleep was a fleeting thing for both Sarah and me as my incessant scratching kept both of us awake. I did develop some really awesome, creepily thick fingernails on my thumbs and pointer fingers during this period, though.

Around this same time I began to cough. I thought to start with it was just a cold, or possibly a consequence of an ear infection. But then it stayed. And stayed. And got worse. And worse.

By Thanksgiving my family finally talked me into doing something I hadn't done since I was a teenager: they convinced me to go to the doctor. And what an enlightening experience it was. We went to an urgent care clinic where I was promptly diagnosed with scabies, a highly contagious burrowing parasite similar to but nastier than head lice. With healthy doses of skepticism and hope we took home our pesticide cream and slathered it all over my body. I still have scars from where it burned my already ravaged flesh. It was hilarious, though, watching Sarah "come down with scabies." Almost nightly she would start uncontrollably itching, which was then followed by, "Do you see this? Does it look like a spot? Or burrow marks?" Ah, the power of suggestion.

I still held out some hope, no matter how small, that the scabies medication would miraculously start working. But then I found Nebraska. Nebraska was the lump under my right arm that I discovered in the shower one day. I named it Nebraska because that was about how big it was. Okay, so in reality it felt closer to a sand dollar both in size and shape, but that's still pretty big for something that's not supposed to be there. Suddenly my hot shower felt very cold. Sure, it could be other things. But any time someone mentions a lump, the first thought that comes up is cancer. Cancer kills people. And it takes insurance or a hefty sum of money to combat it: two things I did not possess.

I also started losing weight. A lot of weight. Like, probably 60 pounds' worth. By the time a third of me disappeared many people started thinking there might really be something wrong with me. If only I hadn't worn that tight Christmas sweater I might have gotten away with it for a while longer.

Christmas drew closer, and as it approached my energy steadily spiraled. The cough also grew increasingly worse until I was coughing so hard and so often that it would make me throw up. A couple of weeks before Christmas I started getting night sweats, and then the week before Christmas I started getting fevers. I would get two to three a day. I didn't completely mind the fevers, though, because when I had them I didn't itch and I didn't cough. I just slept. Who knew a fever could offer such relief?

The Monday before Christmas Eve I was dealing with a fever, and did something I had done possibly only one other time in all the years I had worked at my job: I called in sick. Or, rather, I told them I would come in as soon as I got the fever under control. My pastor and employer's wife, Pastor Joel, who also happens to be a registered nurse, called me back to find out what was going on. After talking with me for a few minutes, she convinced me to go to the ER.

So the day before Christmas Eve we trekked into the emergency room. They thought Nebraska was a fatty tumor and that the itching probably wasn't a big deal. They gave me a cough medicine that didn't work, took a CT scan they didn't see anything on, and sent me on my way.

But then the ER doctor left me a message on Christmas Eve and told me to call her right away. Morning or night, holiday or not. I didn't get the message until midway through Christmas, and by then I figured what's one more day? The news would be the same regardless of a few hours.

The next day I talked to the doctor. She told me that she in fact had not received the actual report from the CT scan until after I had been discharged, and that the full diagnostic was really rather engrossing. She was forwarding me over to one of their cancer doctors, because this definitely looked like an advanced form of lymphoma.

Wondering and Grateful

As 2013 slips farther behind us and 2014 is bursting out all over our madcap lives, I find myself overcome by and beside myself with an overwhelming sense of gratitude. Not just thankfulness: I believe that thankfulness is what we feel when we're given a really good movie or a cutting-edge gadget. Gratefulness is what we feel when we wouldn't have made the house payment this month without that person's help. Gratefulness is when our child steps in front of a moving vehicle and some unknown hero shoves her out of harm's way. These are maybe extreme examples, but I think they illustrate my point: thankfulness comes more from the lips. Gratefulness comes more from the gut.

Why have I felt this gratefulness so intensely? Part of it is because I have been dealing with health issues these past few months. For some reason these problems have not sent me spiraling into a whining, "woe-is-me" state, but really just the opposite: everything has a fresh significance to it. A new importance and vitality. I find my emotions towards things that are beautiful, wondrous and sacrificial to have been heightened exponentially. And perhaps that has led me to my other thoughts.

I've been thinking about the king of the world who was

born an illegitimate child to an unmarried mother. Even though he was embraced by his mother's fiancé, there was never really a question as to whether he was his or not. During a time when adultery (as this would have been seen) was punishable by stoning, he had been ruled unwanted and unworthy of life. If the voices of society had their way, he would have been conveniently disposed of. He was born not in a hospital or even a house, but in a cave surrounded by animal dung and wet straw. He was ushered into a family not of privilege, but of poverty and enslavement. He was hunted. He was oppressed. He was not the sort of person that people wrote limitless volumes of literature or grand epics about like the Greek heroes: in the world's eyes he was destined to be forgotten. But he was and is the King of the world.

I've been thinking about a man, solitary and alone, who was abandoned by every friend he had and executed cruelly — not because he had to be, but because he knew that there was no one else in the entire world who could stand in his place. I've been thinking about a man who saw his brothers drowning in the mire, and dove in with them — not just to be able to commiserate with their suffering, but to pull them up out of it and show them a better way.

I've been thinking about Perfect Love dying for his beloved.

Every day we are looking for a superhero. Someone who will be bigger than us, stronger than us, and do the things that we cannot. The superhero is not a myth. He is real. He is a champion for all people: for the unborn and unwanted, because he himself was unborn and unwanted. For the poor and oppressed, because he was as well. For the broken, sick and lost, because he was the healer and the light in the darkness. For the low in spirit, because he could lift them up. For the thirsty and hungry, because he offered food and drink that were worth far more than a meal. For the distressed and the dying, because he would go to the ends of the earth and beyond to save them. He would even conquer death to give them the chance of new life.

The superhero exists. Believe it. He is called Messiah, Christ, Hero. He is called Jesus of Nazareth.

I am broken. I am empty and I am sick. But in that desperate state I find myself saved by a superhero who is willing to cross Heaven and earth to find me, to sacrifice his life for mine, and to rise again, brilliant and regal, as the King of Creation. And beyond all of that, He is willing to lift me up out of the mire and give me a home in His Kingdom of gold. I tremble in wonder, awe and incredible gratefulness before Him. And I know He will do the same for you. In fact, he already has. All you have to do is believe it.

In recent weeks I've found myself weeping uncontrollably. It has overtaken me at strange times and in inconvenient places. But I weep because greater love has no man than this, that he would lay down his life for his friend. The God of the universe considered me worth enough to be called His friend, and to die so I might live. And for this I am immeasurably grateful.

The Cancer Journal
Part Two

Did I mention that Sarah broke her toe?

It was late Christmas night. I was lying on the couch fighting a fever, trying to convince Sarah to go to sleep. She assured me that she would get back up if she heard me coughing, and I told her that I would be just fine. Finally she begrudgingly headed off to bed, and I fell asleep. An hour or two later, though, I started coughing.

"I'm coming, Byron!" Sarah cried. Lunging out from under

the covers, she raced through our bedroom, skidded around the corner, and –

Thud.

Her eyes grew wide. And then she screamed.

Whether she had run into the door jamb or the refrigerator is irrelevant. In either case she had felt bones move that weren't supposed to.

"I'm okay! I'm okay!" she said as I stumbled over to help her. "No I'm not! No I'm not!" she retorted as we moved her to a chair.

Several weeks (yes, that's right: weeks) later she finally went in for x-rays at her chiropractor's. He looked at the images and chuckled in that way people do while watching a hilarious video where the star probably just broke his hip. "This is awesome!" he proclaimed. "I mean, I am so sorry. But this is awesome!"

And so we entered January.

We got insurance as soon as it was available for ludicrously cheap and allowed pre-existing conditions (thanks, Obamacare!) then met with Dr. Jorges Chaves, the cancer doctor, and his nurse practitioner, Amy Lynes. Dr. Chaves was very quiet, sweet, and restrained. Amy was just the opposite: a wise-cracking bundle of energy. We thoroughly liked them both. Dr. Chaves ordered a bevy of tests, and we set out to accomplish them all. The most memorable one was definitely the bone marrow biopsy. If you have never had the pleasure of undergoing a bone marrow biopsy, let me assure you it is the most unique pain I have ever encountered. I actually felt the vial's worth of bone and goo leave my body, and it did *not* want to go.

When all was said and done we met up with Dr. Chaves again. The skin and bone biopsies had come back blessedly negative. However, the PET scan was a very different matter. My chest and abdominal cavity blazed like a radiant angel from the pit of hell. There was also a node growing on one of my lungs, and there were a lot of warning signs coming from my spleen. Basically my torso had become cancer party zone, and all their friends were invited. Dr. Chaves then said the words that are as close to a punch in the gut as words can get: I had stage four Hodgkin's Lymphoma. There were positives and negatives to this. First of all, it was about as common as cancers get. It was also aggressive, which was ironically a good thing. My youth was another positive. On the other hand, for a variety of reasons I was classified as high risk. The cancer was very advanced. It was aggressive, which was also a bad thing. And my youth was furthermore a negative. Dr. Chaves, in his most gentle and optimistic way, said that statistically we had about a 50% chance of beating the cancer into remission.

That drive back from the doctor was one of the darkest moments (if not the very darkest) of Sarah's and my lives. We had known it was bad, but now the weight of the words "stage four" pressed down on us like anvils. Pastor Joel accompanied us to that appointment, and on the drive back she asked us what we were thinking; what we were most afraid of. For the first time it hit me that I might not get to see my daughters grow up. That it was possible I wouldn't be there for my wife and girls. I'm normally good about fighting off thoughts like that, but on this trip I couldn't escape this particularly monstrous "What if?"

Sarah wanted us to get a second opinion, so we slogged through the traffic up to Seattle. The doctor was very nice, but we realized just how positive a person Dr. Chaves was.

The Seattle doc, Doctor Smith, thought the chances of us killing the cancer were extremely slim, and lobbied that we take an extremely dangerous, highly damaging treatment called Baycop. It was all the rage in Germany, but in the US it was seen as so vicious that its use was practically unheard of. I was one of three people that he had recommended take the treatment in seven years. It would hospitalize me, decimate my bone marrow, make me sterile, destroy my immune system, and do potentially permanent damage to my heart and lungs, but it would definitely wipe out the cancer. We decided to take the treatment that only might do all these things, rather than the one that certainly would.

As we moved out of January and started treatment, I came to a number of conclusions. First of all, most people have no idea how to talk to individuals with diseases or health problems. We don't know how to handle sickness and infirmity. I can't count how many people would come up to Invalid Byron, brace themselves in some way, and, in hushed tones, whisper, "How are you *doing*?" Second, I realized that, no matter how difficult it is for you to accept it, sometimes you won't survive without the help of others. We probably wouldn't have, especially without some who went above and beyond like Sarah's mom, Pam, and my aunt, Julie. Third, I learned that sometimes our plans unfold in funny ways. I had felt for years like big things were going to happen when I hit thirty, and that it would really be the year that launched me into writing and doing what God had purposed for me to do. But instead I was going into the year flat on my back with stage four cancer.

But most of all I came to the conclusion that I was going to come through this, and I was going to bring other people with me. I was not going to just get out by the skin of my teeth: I was going to use this for God and His Kingdom.

And if, in the end, I was able to touch just one life, then by God it would all be worth it.

I truly believe that it was this last conclusion that opened the door for all of the miracles that followed. And follow they did.

Dare to Hope

Do you feel it pulsing just beneath the surface? The panic, the anxiety, the sense that everything is wrong and you don't know how to fix it? The growing, suffocating, crushing weight? Sure, it can be covered up with cheerfulness, laughter and the obligatory "I'm doing just fine, thanks." But that only masks the problem. It's still simmering, waiting to bubble up and clench your heart in its icy grip. You know it's there. And you have no idea what to do about it.

I recently ordered a license plate frame for my car. The message on it states "There is Hope for you. Don't give up." Not real flashy, not overly spiritual, but for me this message triggers something deep and primal. I think this is because, for so many of us, hope is a very small thing: it feels intangible, distant and almost ethereal when compared to the very present issues piling up all around us. The problems could be something as small as an overloaded week or as large as not knowing how you're going to make your house payment. It could be a battle against thoughts you know aren't true, or it could be wondering if you're heading for divorce. It could be a cold. Or it could be cancer. It doesn't matter: they can all overwhelm and overcome us. In the real world, how can such a frail thing as hope survive against such adversaries?

But perhaps hope is more than our fears have made it out to be. Or maybe it's really just a matter of where the hope comes from.

We live in a materialistic culture that prizes what we can see and feel and experience. I mean this in the sense of the "materialism" worldview, i.e. the belief system that acknowledges only things that we can interact with, that are here in front of us, that we can measure and touch. Now, chances are most of the people reading this espouse that there are things beyond this material realm, but no matter your beliefs I guarantee that if you live in the Western world you have been affected by the mindset of materialism. When you're sick you rely on the doctor. To do something better you rely on the newest technology. When you're feeling down you go to the mall or watch a movie or take to social networks to air your frustrations. It's all around us all the time, and it's only natural that after a while we'd come to be influenced by it. But what about when those things fail? What about when physical things, even people, are no longer enough? What about when life breaks and starts falling to pieces? Then we start losing trust. We start losing faith. And we start losing hope. Not only in the material world we live in, but in the God who we assume has left us to our own devices.

But the thing is, God never left us. He was there all along. We were just too busy to notice.

Job had lost everything. His wealth had been destroyed. His children were dead. His wife had, for all intents and purposes, left him. His body was sick and festering. His friends were accusing him of being a liar and a fraud. He didn't understand why this had happened to him, and he was delirious with grief. The consensus was that God had done this to him, and that God had abandoned him. But even then Job said, "Though he slay me, I will hope in him."[1]

Even in his deepest bitterness and despair Job believed that God would show Himself strong on his behalf. But what happened to Job and his hope in the end? He audibly conversed with God. His battered, beaten frame grazed the unfathomable. Lastly, everything that he had lost was replaced, and more besides. And Job's twilight years outshone his dawn.

Last Fall I found a lump under my arm. Not just a small lump, mind you, but one that seemed to me about the size of a sand dollar. I named it "Nebraska", because it was about as big. I can't say this was the start of the most trying months of my life, but it's as good a breaking-in point as any. As Nebraska joined the other maladies plaguing my body I felt my world shuddering beneath me. The malignant little symptoms built one on top of the other, growing steadily heavier, and I felt myself beginning to buckle under the weight.

Despair lurked behind my eyes, in my skull and in my chest. It pressed on me, pulled me down and tried to smother me. But I never lost hope in my God, my Healer. And He has met me where I am. I am not through yet, but since beginning chemo therapy my only side effect has been fatigue. All of my previous problems have evaporated, and I have not undergone any of the trials that I am supposed to during chemo. When asked what is going on I can only point to God because what I have been experiencing doesn't make any natural sense. And God has used this time to touch lives — lives that I would never have reached otherwise. He has answered my hope. And He will answer yours.

May I exhort you with something? Dare to hope. Dare to believe against all materialistic reason in a God who still works in the world today. Dare to have faith in a man who died over 2,000 years ago and then rose again to live forever. Dare to trust in someone who we can't see or touch but can still feel. It is not too late for you. It is not too late for your family. No matter how dark your world looks, He can shine His light and banish your nightmare. No matter how hopeless life appears, He can restore your dreams and make all things new. No matter how big your problems, hope can be bigger if it's in the right Person. "Some trust in chariots and some in horses, but we trust in the name of the Lord our God. They collapse and fall, but we rise and stand upright."[2]

There is Hope for you. Don't give up.

Beauty in the Rain

Oftentimes when it begins to rain I will decide it is time to go for a walk. I will put on my coat and my hat, and as everyone else flees indoors I will step out into the downpour and tumult to begin the trek down our long gravel driveway. I smell the freshly cleaned air, I hear the rain colliding with the leaves, the branches, the road, and I feel the beauty of something greater than me. I find myself filling with awe, consumed by wonder. I become aware of the Father's hand wrapping around me, guiding me, guarding me. As I turn the corner I sense the whisper of

God in my ear, understand the two-way nature of prayer. And I realize that everyone else ran inside to get away from this.

Don't get me wrong: I know that the rain is wet and cold and at times even oppressive. I understand why people would want to avoid it. I even do myself sometimes. But I also think that by not stepping out into the rain, by not taking that chance of getting wet, we sometimes miss out on the beauty that is as fresh as a glistering raindrop on a flower.

I'm sure it's not hard to see where I'm going with this, but nevertheless I'm going there anyway. How often have we not seen the very best in our lives because we've been afraid to go out in the rain? How often do we, in an effort to avoid the uncomfortable, forsake the very thing God intended to use to unleash His glory?

Of course, a lot of the time we have no choice about whether we are going out into the dark, the storm, the unknown. Many times there are just no other options. Even still, how we deal with our tempest from the outset can determine where our journey will ultimately end up.

When we're in that darkness and that cold, are we looking for the little glimmers of glory? When that proposition stares us in the face and it scares us to death, are we nonetheless strong enough to embrace it anyway?

Hananiah, Mishael and Azariah (better known by their slave names Shadrach, Meshach and Abednego) were stabbed in the back by the jealous wizards and philosophers who attended with them in the king's court. Soon the king offered them a choice: they could bow and worship the golden image he had set before them, or they could be burned alive in a furnace of unimaginable fury. The three young men, however, did not waver. With steely eyes they looked their king in the face and as one voice declared: "Our God whom we serve is able to deliver us from the burning fiery furnace, and he will deliver us out of your hand, O king. But if not, be it known to you, O king, that we will not serve your gods or worship the golden image that you have set up." The king raged and ordered them thrown into the inferno. Hananiah, Mishael and Azariah were bound hand and foot, and then they were tossed into the blazing furnace. With a self-satisfied smirk the king peered down at his handiwork. He gasped. "Did we not cast three men bound into the fire?" he asked. "But I see four men unbound, walking in the midst of the fire, and they are not hurt; and the appearance of the fourth is like a son of the gods!"[3]

Their dark night of the soul came with fire. What did yours come with? And, more importantly, how will you choose to answer it?

We were never promised "the good life," pain-free and divorced from suffering. Just the opposite, in fact: we were promised trials and tribulations. But the question then becomes, what are we going to do about those things? Will we run from them, hide our faces and bemoan our fate? Or will we choose to see the beauty glimmering all around us? Hananiah, Mishael and Azariah changed a nation with their resolve, and in so doing they also met a man who was "like a son of the gods." Who knows: maybe you will, too.[4]

Coauthoring Our Destinies

How much input do we have over our own destinies?

Or, rather, how integral a part do we play in determining our little segment of the cosmic story?

One man feels like he is called by God to change a nation. So he goes and, with God's help, he does it. Did he have a choice in following the call? Or was he always destined for greatness?

Another man leaves his wife and baby and hops on a train

with no destination in mind. A third one gets in a fight and ends up running from the cops. Did they take paths they were scripted to run down? Or did they have a hand in writing these dramas for themselves?

When Abraham talked to God and implored Him to save Sodom and Gomorrah if he found but ten righteous people, had God already decided that He would give Abraham what he wanted? Was it all prewritten? Or did Abraham change God's mind?[5]

Why was God horrified to find that Cain had killed Abel?[6] Why would He give nations the chance to repent if there was no chance they would?[7]

How much control do we have over our lives? Any? Some? All?

Maybe this all sounds a little too lofty and academic. But try these phrases on for size: "Everything happens for a reason." "It's all part of God's plan." "Why did God allow this?"

How many times have you heard someone say one of those phrases? How many times have you said them yourself? I'm not necessarily here to prove them wrong (though I'm definitely not here to prove them right), but I want you to see that this isn't just a dusty academic issue. This is something that affects us all. And it distinctly affects how we see God.

As a writer, I have always been very attracted to the idea of God as the Author and Finisher of our faith. It is very easy for me to see God as the great creator; the consummate, ultimate storyteller. I think that there is great truth in this: looking back at my life, I can see the plot lines winding and weaving and intersecting. I can see how this led to this which led to this, and that I would not be the person I am today if any of these things had been different. That includes the good and the bad.

However, I feel there is another side, too. I don't think God is only interested in being the Great Author. I don't even think He's interested in just being the main character (for more on this, see Jesus.) I think he wants to be a collaborator. And I think He wants His fellow collaborator to be you.

For millions of years God spun out his story, his drama, his artistic and creative masterpiece called the universe. He spoke and light, matter and energy exploded into existence. He forged a breathtaking panoply of particles and lit the dark with supernovae and swirled clouds of dust into planets. It was mind-numbingly stunning. But it was all in preparation for what was to come. Up until that point He had written the story by Himself. But now He had formed a stage and the raw materials necessary for the coauthors to emerge, and to join in the creating.

And we did. Each one of us was given a few years (barely a flicker in the cosmic history) to write our own tales. And then our part would be done, and another would take our place. We could help to shape the Great Story, for good or ill, as we saw fit. God would maintain overall creative control, of course, but He was also incredibly generous with His narrative.

Sometimes we did the right thing, and the symphony achieved a rousing high note. Often we did not, and the chronicles plunged into darkness and depths of despair. Quite often we even crafted in shades of horror.

But here's the crux of it: I believe that we have license to shape the story. I believe that our destinies remain unfulfilled not because God didn't really mean for greatness to happen to us, but because we never did anything about it. We are so busy waiting for God to write something interesting, when He's really saying, "This is your piece. You write it."

I know a man who loves God. And every time I talk to him, he is anxiously looking forward to the day when God finally tells him how to apply his talents and make a difference for the Kingdom. He's not a spring chicken any more. But any day now, he's pretty sure God is going to tell him what to do and where to go. And when that day comes, boy will it be great to know what God intends for him.

What if he reaches the end of his life and God never tells him what to do? Or what if God did, and he just never listened? What if God was telling him to write his own story?

I don't claim that this is an exhaustive answer, or even a particularly good one. It's just something I've been thinking about, and I am certainly open to greater knowledge and new ideas. But for now, I would love for you to think on this: if God gave you the outline and you're filling in the details, what details would you want to see in your life? At the end of your days what would make you feel like you made a difference and changed the world? What would send ripples through future storytellers for generations to come?

Go. Write that.

The Cancer Journal
Part Three

We went into treatment. Prior to starting, though, we were told the laundry list of side effects. These included, but were not limited to:

- Nerve Damage
- Heart Damage
- Lung Damage

- Severe Fatigue
- Demolished White Blood Cell Counts
- Demolished Red Blood Cell Counts
- Trashed Immune System
- Nausea
- Vomiting
- Diarrhea
- Constipation
- Loss of Appetite
- Acid Indigestion
- Hair Loss
- Fevers
- Mouth Sores
- Unpleasant Metallic Taste in Mouth

Now, these were not necessarily possible side effects: I was guaranteed to have two- to three-quarters of these.

The first couple treatments passed, and I was still doing pretty well. But it didn't stay that way. Around the third or fourth treatment I was hit by excruciating acid indigestion. It was so bad that I could barely function. It raged inside my guts, ripping apart my insides. The one tiny acid indigestion pill they had prescribed I take daily wasn't touching it. We talked to Dr. Chaves, and he advised me to start taking two of them a day. If that didn't work, we'd look at something stronger.

The next day I was in prayer around noon at work/church. The thought occurred to me that just because everyone else had to go through this stuff didn't mean I did. So I prayed against the acid indigestion and thanked God for taking it away. Immediately I felt it fading. And then I didn't feel anything. Furthermore, though there was a little bit that would flare up now and again over the coming months, that intense acid never came back. In fact, I reached the point where I pretty much stopped taking the acid pill altogether (though I would take it for a few days whenever I was chided by medical professionals.)

A similar thing happened with my blood counts and immune system. I was anemic when I went into treatment, so I was already off to a bad start. The threat of infusions was very real and often present. However, when I would get the panicked phone call telling me my counts had been flushed down the toilet, people would pray for me and the next time they would always have made a valiant rebound.

The best part, though, was the lives we touched. We soon learned that our favorite nurse, Debbie, was not only a Christian but that she attended the church renting from my church. When she learned who I was her eyes got really big and she exclaimed, "Oh! You're the one we've been making meals and praying for!" Small world, huh? We further made friendships with Deb (no relation to Debbie,) Rita, and a number of the other chemo patients. We had opportunities to pray for many of them and talk about God. Sarah actually did far more than me in these regards, as we quickly learned that intravenous Benadryl knocks me out faster than a skillet to the skull. Because of this, I ended up sleeping through good chunks of my treatments.

As we continued on, too, a funny thing happened. Or, rather, didn't happen. My major symptoms I had going into chemo (the coughing, the itching, etc.) faded to nothing after the first few weeks. And all of the other side effects we'd been promised never manifested (with the exception of fatigue.) I had been told that I would want to stop eating. But on the contrary, I started eating more. I was guaranteed to get this weird flavor that would flood my mouth and change the taste of food no later than the third or fourth treatment. That also failed to happen. Sure, I got a faint metallic taste in my mouth near the tale-end, but it was so minor that I don't know that I ever even told Sarah. (Surprise, Sarah!) In fact, there were some weeks where the taste became sweet. And the vomiting, nausea, diarrhea, constipation, et al? They didn't show up, either.

I did begin losing my hair en masse, which led to one really entertaining bath (complete with heart-warming "Eeew! What have you done to my tub?" from my wife.) Following this we decided to just shave my head. But then another curious event occurred: my hair started growing again as soon as we cut it off. This happened two more times, though each time there was less hair that fell out. My eyebrows were not so lucky, unfortunately. There are still two or three robust, courageous hairs sticking in there, but that's about it.

After a while I learned how expensive my medication was, so I stopped taking it (excepting the acid pill whenever I was told I'd get an ulcer otherwise.) This added to the conversations I would have at every doctor appointment, which I memorized:

They would say, "How are you?"

I would say, "Doing great."

They would say, "What new side effects do you have?"

I would reply, "None."

They would say, "Any nausea, diarrhea or constipation?"

I would say, "Nope."

They would counter, "Are you sure?"

"Yep."

"Any tingling in your fingers or toes?" (A sign of nerve damage.)

"No."

"What medications do you need refilled?"

"None."

"Really? Why?"

"Because I haven't needed to take any of them."

"What do you mean?"

"I haven't had any side effects."

I came to love it when people would approach me to talk to Invalid Byron (as mentioned in Part Two.) When they would start into how sorry they were for me or talking in the hushed tones, I would reply with "Actually, I'm doing pretty great. God's really blessing." It was wonderful to see the conversation immediately flip around. The person contacted me lamenting: the person left glorifying God and filled with hope. Finally I started asking people who wanted to pray with me if they would instead pray that we would have the opportunity to change other's lives. It seems whenever I got someone to pray this we had great encounters the following week.

Treatments continued to roll past, and we approached the four-month mark where we would take a new PET scan and reassess the situation. I went in for the scan, and when it was over I tried to thank the technician. He had done my original PET scan, and he remembered me from the previous visit (he also remembered that I worked in a church, interestingly enough.) This was why it was strange that he didn't acknowledge me at all as I was leaving. He just kept looking at my scans with a scowl on his face. I felt a creeping dread enter me. What was he seeing on my scans?

There is Peace

The little boat flailed as thunder cracked the skies and lightning lit the clouds. The waves thrashed and writhed like children on a temper tantrum as panic crawled down the crewmen's throats and gripped their guts. Turning to their leader, the bedraggled sailors cried out, "Master, Master, we are perishing!"

Why did they have to yell at him so? Wasn't it obvious what was happening? Apparently not, because their master was in the back of the boat asleep.[8]

How could he have been asleep? Didn't he know they were dying? Did he not care?

How many times do we assume God is asleep? Or away on vacation? This is one of the ideas raised in the book "The Sunflower" by Simon Wiesenthal, a true story from Nazi-controlled Poland about the limits of forgiveness and the lives of Jews in concentration camps.[9] Life was so hellish for the people of the camps that several of them began to champion the position that God was on leave. The question – has God abandoned us – hangs heavy and unanswered in the air, a pendulous weight on the book's pages. It, along with the other questions the book more prominently asks about forgiveness and love in the most evil of circumstances, haunts you long after you have finished the book (which I highly recommend you read.)

So is and was it true? Was God absent? Does the Master not care?

One of only two characters who can be said to keep his faith in "The Sunflower" is also the only Christian. Why did he keep his faith when the Jews almost unanimously lost it? Perhaps it is partly because the Christian faith has a critical leg up on its Jewish forebear in that every time we read the gospels we see where God is amidst suffering: nailed to a cross, bruised, beaten and bloody. He isn't somewhere far off when we suffer; he is right there suffering with us.

But obviously there is a different reason Jesus was asleep while everyone else was screaming and scrabbling to life. They were consumed by fear and panic. But he was filled with something else entirely: the miracles of faith and peace. The kind that can cause a person to sleep through a tempest.

There is a beautiful song called "There is Peace" which I have sung in choir. The chorus is: "There is peace in Jesus, there is rest in His will. And when we trust Him to lead us, our hearts can be still." That same peace Jesus felt in the boat is available to us. Why? Because we have a good Daddy, and a faithful big brother who will never leave us or forsake us. They stand with us in affliction. They accompany us in the storm. And they offer us shelter from the barrage of life.

Where are you right now? Are you in the dark? Are you in the storm? Are you being buffeted by the wind and the waves and the terror that this will all end in destruction? Embrace Jesus. Ask for His peace. Tell Him where you're at and how much rope you have left. (Including if you're at the end of it.) And then take a deep breath, close your eyes, and let "the peace of God, which surpasses all understanding,"[10] consume you.

Trials come and trials go. Trust me, I know all about that. But the peace that surpasses understanding can remain. When we lean into our Creator, when we stay in that place of trust, every time fear rears its vile head we can take a deep breath, feel Jesus wrap his arms around us, and dissolve our cares in the ocean of his Care. Is it always easy? No, I won't lie and say that it is. But it's always worth it.

Cross-Stitched Lives

Just over ten years ago essentially every deep, lifelong friend I'd had walked away from me and my family. They did this because the group of churches I had grown up in told them to, and they were informed that anyone who talked to us would be tossed out along with us.

With a couple of exceptions, I haven't talked to them since.

I hadn't thought about most of them in quite some time, to be honest. But this week a dream brought them all back to my memory. I felt the hole that they had left afresh. I remembered the good, and I remembered the bad. And I started thinking about the impact each of us has on the lives of those around us.

Why do we meet the people we do, make the friends we have, lose the ones we don't any more? Is it for any particular reason? Are we all just bumping into each other at random, like blind forces of nature impacting one another? Does chance decide where we live and where we were born and who we were born to?

I don't think so. I think our moments form a deliberate pattern.

We weave in and out of each other's lives, adding to one another as we go. Some of us cross paths for only a few seconds. Others are intertwined for fifty years. In the end, though, just as we came together, we will eventually part. It is inevitable, at least in this life. But perhaps, rather than dwelling on the parting as we are so wont to do, we should instead ask what we are adding to each other while we're together.

When we are joined to another person's life are we sewing joy or tragedy? Are we building up the people we meet, or tearing them down? Do we exist only for ourselves and consequently bring pain? Or do we exist for others and bring renewal?

And when we part, what do we focus on? Do we see only the bad? The dark? The twisted little memories that perhaps drove us apart in the first place? Or do we focus on the good? Do we see how this person's life changed us, how they made us better, and strive to live for that memory?

Really, I think that most of the time it's the events that are incredibly negative in the present that most shape us into the people we are becoming. If ultimately these events strengthen us, then I think that even these things we must be thankful for – perhaps more so than the positive times. Was it hard while you were going through it? Undoubtedly. Does it still hurt to this day? Perhaps. But would you really want to go back to who you were before?

So many of us walk around in a near-constant state of brokenness, shattered by the lives that have crashed into ours. And so often it is the people closest to us who have the greatest opportunity to break us into a million pieces. Why are you holding onto that pain? What good is it doing you? Is it worth it, to live in that place of ebony emptiness? Wouldn't it be better to let the dazzling brilliance of Jesus flood that area and bring you fullness? Maybe you've even said you've forgiven the other person. But isn't it time that you said it and meant it? I am certain there were good times with that person as well, because otherwise you wouldn't have been so hurt by them. What if you remembered only those and let go of the rest?

I hold nothing against any of my old friends. In fact, what I did when I started thinking about them again was to pray for them. I hope for only the best for all of them. Some day I would be thrilled to tell them that in person.

We each are woven together for a time, and then our strands move off. But while we're together, why not work to change the other person's life for the better? Why not strive to make every life we come in contact with enriched for having met us? What can we do to change them, and consequently to change the world?

So often we're looking for our Big Purpose. For the Grand Meaning. Now, don't get me wrong, I fully believe there is a purpose meant for each of us (if we will allow it.) But maybe sometimes we're trying too hard. Maybe sometimes all we really have to do is let go of the dark, and give someone the light. Maybe we just need to make sure every thread that is stitched together with ours leaves us a little brighter.

We only have one chance to weave this magnificent mosaic called life. What do you say we make the most of it?

This Island, Man

When you can no longer interact with people according to socially acceptable norms you begin to cultivate a unique perspective on society. It can be so easy to feel like an island, even when you're surrounded by continent. You're in the throng, people are milling about all around you happy and talking and laughing, but you're still completely isolated. You can stand amidst hundreds of others and still be utterly alone.

I've been through this recently on both sides of the

aisle. On the one hand, I went for months when I had a compromised immune system, so I was forced to wear a surgical mask and this little personal air purifier that had a flashing LED on it. (Which I'm still thankful for, by the way – you're the best, Aunt Julie!) The air purifier drew looks and comments, but it was much better than the alternative: the surgical mask. Maybe in other cultures wearing surgical masks is a perfectly normal, acceptable social behavior. But in America, people look at you – and treat you – like you are currently carrying Bird Flu. This doesn't improve once they actually talk to you and learn that you have cancer. As I've mentioned before, Americans do not know how to talk to sick people. So instead they hem and haw and slink away as quickly as they gracefully can.

On the other hand, I was recently at a concert with my brother (to see the grand maestros of "Showbread" – may raw rock kill you forever and ever, amen.) As we were sitting there waiting for the show to start, a girl came up behind us and asked if the seat next to me was saved for anyone. I said it was reserved for her, she said, "Cool," and sat down next to me. As the minutes stretched on I realized that just about everyone else was talking with friends and having a good time, but this girl was all alone. She didn't look at all like the type of person who fit in this crowd (I barely did), and I started wondering what her story was and what had brought her to this show. I started trying to come up with a way to open up a conversation with her, but I couldn't think of anything that wouldn't make me look like I was a creeper, making moves, or just weird. (I'm an introvert, all right? I realize there were all sorts of perfectly acceptable things I could have said, but for some reason at that moment nothing was coming.) Finally the concert got going and I got off the hook. But then later on the lead singer said that the only reason the band still existed after all these years was because of Jesus. Just about everyone in the crowd went crazy. Except for this girl.

Am I making too much of this? Maybe. Probably, even. But as we left that night, I couldn't help but wonder if I had missed out on an opportunity to touch her life. And I wondered if she had remained an island because no one had invited her to join the mainland.

Actor Robin Williams died recently of an apparent suicide. Many have said he was in the midst of a deep depression. It would seem even fame, money, and fans don't cure us of our loneliness. In fact, in Mr. Williams' case, I wonder if it made it worse; if being surrounded by so many who wanted a piece of him, criticized him and idolized him made him more alone than ever.

Which of these are you? Are you on the island looking in? Or are you on the continent glancing out? I'm going to guess it's been a bit of both.

It can be so easy to become an army of one. Don't let it happen. Don't let isolation envelope your life. You weren't meant to journey through this world alone: you were meant to influence and be influenced by others. Do others shun us or not understand us or talk behind our backs? Sure. But we are the ones who choose to let that burn us. We are the ones who decide to rise above the dirt or be buried by it. We can either overcome or be overcome: the choice is ours. It's so easy to make our church a TV preacher or a streaming service online, and skip the human connection altogether. It's so convenient to make our social lives Facebook rather than face-to-face. I'm not saying any of these things are wrong in and of themselves, but when they become our Wilson[11] we have a serious issue.

And then there's the flip-side of the coin. A stranger walks into your social sphere and you suddenly find yourself at a crossroad. It's so much more comfortable to carry on as you were. It's far less trying to pretend you don't see her and let her pass. And chances are there will be no skin off your back for doing just that. But what if you are the one and only glimmer of light she will see? What if your comfort is consigning her to darkness? It's easy to brush off that thought as silly or severe. But how do you know? What if that social misfit is in a place as dark as Mr. Williams, and a word from you could save his life? What if the wall flower just desperately needs to know she matters and that she's beautiful? What if the outcast hungers deep in his soul to be told that he finally belongs? How can we ever be salt and light if we never let anyone taste or see?

Ironically, it is incredibly easy in this connected age to find yourself that solitary island. But we were never supposed to be. You were meant for so much more. Have you been hurt before? Burned? Cast off? Welcome to the human race. But, to paraphrase/quote Rob Bell, the question is where will we go from there? Will we be bitter or better? Closed or open? More ignorant or more aware?[12] We choose if we stay out in the cold, and we can choose if others do as well.

May we choose warmth.

The Cancer Journal
Part Four

Two days passed following the PET scan. I tried to push the technician's look out of my mind, but without much success. And so we came to Friday evening. I was driving when the doctors' office called, and because I didn't want to "break the law" I didn't answer it. Good excuse, no? If you don't want to hear bad news right away, just send them to voice mail because you're driving! Mad props, state patrol!

When we parked, though, I finally screwed up the courage

to listen to the message. Amy's voice came on the phone. But she didn't sound morose: instead she sounded ecstatic. She said, "Hi, Byron, this is Amy from Dr. Chaves's office. I just couldn't wait until next week to give you the good news. The PET scan looks fabulous. We can't see any cancer, anywhere… We'll go over the PET scan in detail when we see you, but there has been complete resolution of all of the hot spots… So you and the Good Lord doing all that great work, congratulations, and you guys have a fabulous weekend!"

I sat there, dumbfounded. And then I chuckled.

Sarah said, "What did she say? Play it for me!" So I replayed it on loudspeaker.

Can I tell you the strangest part of this whole evening? It was that we didn't start jumping up and down or shouting right away. Instead, we almost felt sober. Sounds weird, doesn't it? But the truth was that we'd been having such a great time and touching so many lives that we didn't want it to end. However, I saw the hand of God all over this. And I knew from experience that we had to lean into Him and trust Him, just like we had so many times before.

I told Sarah as much. Slowly we allowed ourselves to start getting excited and to step once again into the unknown. And we started planning how to tell people. Because the thing everyone had been praying for had happened: I had been healed.

How can I definitively say that I had been healed by God? Good question. Here's the part that rankles me: I can't. I can only go on the evidence presented to me and infer from that the best answer. But here's the evidence: no one expected me to be over the cancer at four months. Not the doctors, not me, not the PET tech. Had it happened before? Sure. But it was extremely rare. Especially for high risk, stage four dudes with dangerously advanced symptoms. And despite my good attitude, I don't think there's any way that was enough. Plus, the fact is that we don't know when the cancer actually died. It could have been at three months. Or even two. We just don't know.

Second of all, there are all of the little miracles that happened leading up to this. From the acid miracle to the blood counts to the lack of side effects to all of the other little things that added up to be one big thing along the way.

Third, there are the other lives that have been impacted. I will get into this a little bit later, but there has been at least one healing following mine that was a direct result of my testimony and of people praying. Jim had been trying for years to get his thyroid to work properly. And is it coincidence that the week after he heard my testimony, when I specifically told him that he was next, he suddenly had a normally functioning thyroid and began weaning himself off of the medication he had been on for years? Not just because he suddenly felt fine, but also because his doctor said so? That stretches incredulity past the breaking point, in my opinion.

But in the end, this, like so much of life, has to be taken a little bit on faith. Having said that, when you combine the evidence I mentioned above with my faith, I can tell you that, yes, without a doubt, God healed me of stage four Hodgkin's Lymphoma. Was it instantaneous as so many expect a miracle to be? No. But, honestly, I wouldn't have missed out on these experiences for the world. And God's not done yet.

Throughout our treatment God used many people to bless

us in a multitude of ways. But a more common way we were blessed was through the gift of money. It started coming in while we were still in chemo mode. But it really started coming in once we decided to trust God and start stepping out of chemo mode. I can now say that, through many wonderful, generous people (and one in particular who will remain anonymous for now), we are coming out of this free of medical debt — something that I never could have imagined was possible back in December. But God's not done yet.

Through my testimony I have been told by many that they now believe in miracles again. That they now believe God is still at work in the world today. I told our nurse, Debbie, that I was cancer free. She looked at me, dead serious, and said, "Thank you so much for telling me. We don't get to hear that much around here." I told four ladies in a Panera that I had been healed of cancer. They turned out to be Thailand missionaries who also work with Women's Aglow (now Aglow International.) By the time we were done talking they could barely sit in their chairs. (In fact, they didn't: they all jumped up and descended on ours.) For me there could be no greater gift. And I am not the last. This makes me cry out once again in wonder and gratefulness to the Father of Life. The superhero does exist. And if he chose to pull me out of the burning building in front of hundreds of observers, so be it. He's not done yet.

Oh, and remember previously when I mentioned that I thought my thirtieth year would be the year I started stepping out into what God had put me on this earth for? It turns out I was right. God has used this cancer, from the very first time I wrote about it, to launch me. It has touched lives that I would never have had any contact with. And it has transformed both me, my family, and many, many others. What more could I ask for than that? But

God's not done yet.

This has been a little bit of my story. I hope it has blessed you. I hope it has touched your life and that you will share it with others to touch theirs. Barring that, I hope it has made you think and consider: is there more to existence than I thought there was? Does God still work today? Is there reason to wonder? What if? And, lastly, I pray that the battle-cry on your lips (for yourself, for your circumstance, for your family, for your region, your country and the world,) will be this:

God's not done yet.

Our Healer

I stood in the shower, tears melting into the spray from the shower head on my cheeks. With nothing else to do, I sang (as well as my tortured throat would allow): "I believe you're my healer. I believe you are all I need. I believe you're my portion. I believe you're more than enough for me. Jesus, you're all I need." This was followed with, "Nothing is impossible for you. You hold my world in your hands."[13]

Many days it was all I could do to sing this song, or others like it. But it was enough.

Other days, when I had more strength, I would walk what Mark Batterson calls prayer circles around our house.[14] And that was good, too.

But really, there is very little I did. All I really did was push past the fear and doubt and embrace a stubbornness that God and I were going to win. The hundreds or thousands of people around the world who learned about my condition did much more than me. Their prayers encompassed and blanketed the world, and sent a sweet savor up to Heaven. I know many of us have a tendency to embrace the "If it be thy will" prayers, but I have a hard time believing that many of the people praying for me did this. I believe they went something more like this: "Father, heal him!" Why? First of all, because I know a lot of the people praying for me. But most of all because God did. In four months.

Why was I healed when so many others aren't? What made me special? Was it, as I've been told over and over again, my attitude? Was it because of the way people prayed bold prayers of faith over me? I do know that it was a combination of both of these things, but I've seen people with as much faith or more than me still die from this, and I myself have prayed boldly for someone only to watch them pass away two days after. Was it because of my chemo? Or the vitamins I was taking? Yes, I know that both of these were natural parts of this process. But *no one* was expecting me to be over this in the time it took, if I got over it at all. And how can those things explain the complete lack of side effects I experienced (apart from fatigue)? Another crazy thing? Yes, we learned at the end of four months of treatment that I was cancer-free. But it could have easily happened at three months. Or even two. My cancer-free date of 5/9/14 was just the day that we got the results of our test.

Or was it just not my time to go? Most assuredly it was not, but I've known others who went out when it arguably wasn't their time. (Don't believe that's possible? For a converse of this idea, read about Hezekiah in the Old Testament.[15]) Was it because I never gave up? Surely that was a part of it. I've seen many who gave up and only survived for a few days past that point. They were given a choice, and they took it. Who could fault them for that? However, I don't believe I was ever pushed to that point. People would often come into my office at work and say, "Well, I shouldn't be complaining. Look at what you're going through." And in my head I would say, "You know, this really hasn't been that bad."

So why me? Why have I been chosen when so many others haven't been? (Including some in my own family.)

Can I be honest with you? I think that sometimes people need a rallying point. A lightning rod, if you will. They need the go-ahead to go ahead and believe that they can make it, too.

We've lived in this twilight land for so long that we don't know whether we're moving into daylight or nighttime. We want healing to be true. We want to know that God's promises are as valid today as they were thousands of years ago. But we just don't know. We want to know this God and trust in this God and love this God, but can we? Or should we just get jaded? Do we just give in and call anyone who believes in this stuff a hypocrite or a misled huckster? The evidence seems to mount and mount against healing and the God who says He heals, but deep in our hearts I think we still want it to be true. I think there's a part of us that needs it to be true.

The question, after all, isn't just "does God heal?" The

question is also, "does God love me?"

When we finally knew we were dealing with stage four Hodgkin's Lymphoma and chemotherapy, I determined that I was not going to come through this thing alone. What I mean is, if I could change just one life through this process, if I could show just one person how real Jesus and the Father were through my suffering, then everything else would be worth it. And I believe that's exactly what's happened. God's made me a gateway healing. Come on in.

"By His wounds you have been healed."[16] Do you believe that? Can you believe that? You should. It happened to me. It can happen to you, too. I don't care if it's cancer or an incurable disease or an imbalance in your body or brokenness in your family. God can heal you just as easily as He healed me. Healing wasn't just for the old Apostles. It's happening, today. His stripes heal just as well now as they did back at the first church.

I'm not singing the "Healer" song for me any more. I'm singing it for you. He is our healer. Now it's your turn.

Would you do me two favors? First, share this with someone who needs it. Second of all, tell me what you need prayer for. You can do this either on my website at http://www.lifespringseternal.com, or by email at byron@byronleavitt.com. I would love to pray with you, and if it's okay with you I'd love to get other people praying for you as well. There is a new prayer page on Life Springs that's there for this very purpose.

Let's stand together with some rabid faith and really believe God's as good as His Word. And, by all means, when your healing comes, don't keep it to yourself. Tell me. Tell the world. Scream it from the rooftops.

What do you say we start a movement? I'm down. How about you?

Life Springs Eternal

When was the last time that you thought about death?

Does it sound morbid to say that I think about it a lot?

Now, sure, it's probably natural for someone who's been fighting cancer to think about death somewhat. After all, for many people it is a sharp slap in the face that, contrary to popular opinion, they are probably not the exception to the rule of mortality. But this isn't a new thing for me. I have thought a great deal about death for a very long time. Sometimes it has scared me. Sometimes it has made my faith waver. Because, in the end, we all have to face the Great Dark.

Some people are healed of a deadly disease. Some receive miracles and victories and happiness. But, in the end, every miracle is temporal. Not a one of them lasts forever. Eventually everything — and everyone — turns to dust. Eventually death comes for us all.

And, if the materialist worldview is right, oblivion will swallow each of us up, and that will be our end. There are no happy endings. There is only tragedy.

A couple of years ago I was studying the Old Testament. Imagine my surprise when I discovered that the early Jews felt very similarly to the materialists. Even King David. He didn't believe in an afterlife as we do, but in Sheol: a dark shadow world where people could not truly be said to be alive.[17] His son, Solomon, one of the wisest men in history according to the Bible, said, "Who knows whether the spirit of man goes upward and the spirit of the beast goes down into the earth?"[18] Then, later, he said, "For the living know that they will die, but the dead know nothing, and they have no more reward, for the memory of them is forgotten."[19] Most early Christians did not believe in an afterlife per se, either. They believed in a resurrection of the dead, but until that happened their brothers and sisters slept a sleep only God could wake them from.[20] This was a highly controversial idea even in first century Judaism, though, and it had squarely divided the Levites. Some of them chose to hope in the resurrection (the Pharisees), but the scriptural purists (the Sadducees) did not believe in any such thing.[21] In fact, our idea of Heaven arose mainly from a very interesting source: the Greek philosophers, especially Socrates and Plato.[22]

These realizations brought me to my crisis of faith: not in God, and not in Jesus, but in Heaven. In the afterlife. In the question, "Is there more?" Or were the early Jews right? Would we all, in the end, be devoured by the ravenous Nothing? By the Unending Black?

But then an idea occurred to me. Creation begins in blackness. What if, in the blackness of our oblivion, the Creator was shaping something new?

Around this time I began studying near-death experiences. These stories of people who came back captivated me. They expressed the wonder and the joy of the afterlife that I had lost.[23] I studied consciousness. I strove for a deeper understanding of Heaven.[24] And a spark ignited afresh in me that had previously guttered to embers.

What if there *is* more?

What if there's hope?

What if we desire another life – a better world – for a reason? What if we have heard rumors of eternity because the rumors are true?

Why did Jesus tell the other man on a cross, "Today you will be with me in Paradise"?[25] Was Paul talking about a near-death experience in 2 Corinthians?[26]

What if there's a light at the end of the tunnel?

As our Western culture has become mortified of death, the Christian Church has followed suit. For instance, it is taboo in much of Christian music now to sing about Heaven or what comes after, because we have sanitized our inevitable future and focused solely on the here and now. I'm not saying it's a bad thing to sing of God's everyday grace, but we are doing ourselves a disservice by not imagining the future. We are missing the end of the story. And the end is this:

Every life ends in tragedy, for every life ends in death. Darkness eats away at the vision, the chest gives one final heave and is still. All those hopes, dreams and memories, all the friends, laughter and love, are eradicated in one instant of oblivion. Mourning in a moment swallows joy whole. But then, in the midst of the tragedy, in the macabre stillness, there is a burst of light. The man once dead casts off the shell that has encased him, and rises from the ashes of his spent existence. And so it is that at the final call, the last tolling, when the villain has won, death has swallowed life and all lies dark and wasted, that the Great Author throws one final turn in the story. And suddenly the life, in a blaze of glory, rises anew. Reborn. With a new chance. A new hope. And only then is there the possibility of a happy ending.

A happy ending is really just the chance for a new beginning. Without God there is no new beginning. Without Heaven and the afterlife and the Kingdom there is no victory. And without the Lord Jesus Christ there is no example. Jesus's greatest message of hope wasn't only that he died for our sins. It was that He showed us that it was possible to rise again.

"No chilling wind or poisonous breath

Can reach that healthful shore.

Where sickness, sorrow, pain and death

Are felt and feared no more."[27]

"O death, where is your sting?"[28]

In the end, Life Springs Eternal.

Where We Go From Here

"Hope deferred makes the heart sick."[29] What a placid way to discuss how the venom of disappointment poisons the soul.

Every week I ask God what He wants me to write about on my blog. And every week I get an answer. This week the answer was "disappointment and discouragement." Sometimes I have experiences after learning the theme that help me in writing the post. (This happened with

"This Island, Man.") I'd already been dealing with some disappointment and discouragement, though, so I thought I had my "teaching from experience" story for the week. I was wrong.

We had a doctor's appointment Thursday to go over the results of my last PET scan, where we heard there were indications the cancer was returning. There were only a couple little spots, but that didn't change the fact there were spots. Could they still be something else? Yes. We will biopsy them to make sure, but if they are lymphoma we will be starting down the chemo road once again.

Now, I'll admit, there's a part of me that suspected something was amiss. When we had the CT scan prior to the PET scan, I had a feeling there would be something on it. Not a dread, just an impression. Same with the PET scan. So I can't say I was beside myself with shock. But disappointed? That's a whole other matter.

There's a part of me that thinks, does this mean I wasn't healed? Could I really have been that wrong?

There's a part of me that thinks, it's starting all over again.

There's a part of me, the really tired part, the part that never completely recovered from the last chemo, that's just sighing, wondering what will hit us next. Especially considering everything else I've been dealing with recently. (To protect others I won't go into the rest of my recent disappointments and discouragements. I don't want anyone to get hurt by my words or feelings.)

There's a part of me that wonders if I have misled people in what I've said, in what I've stood for. This is the one that plagues me the most.

So where do we go from here? When the rug's been pulled

out from under us how do we keep moving forward?

How can we even be sure what direction forward is?

We start by reading this.

"Therefore, having this ministry by the mercy of God, we do not lose heart. ... For God, who said, "Let light shine out of darkness," has shone in our hearts to give the light of the knowledge of the glory of God in the face of Jesus Christ.

"But we have this treasure in jars of clay, to show that the surpassing power belongs to God and not to us. We are afflicted in every way, but not crushed; perplexed, but not driven to despair; persecuted, but not forsaken; struck down, but not destroyed; always carrying in the body the death of Jesus, so that the life of Jesus may also be manifested in our bodies. ...

"So we do not lose heart. Though our outer self is wasting away, our inner self is being renewed day by day. For this light momentary affliction is preparing for us an eternal weight of glory beyond all comparison, as we look not to the things that are seen but to the things that are unseen. For the things that are seen are transient, but the things that are unseen are eternal."[30]

I've been reevaluating what I know to be the purpose for my life, and my priorities. I've been taking a second look at what's happened to me the past few months. I've been working to forgive those who have hurt me. And I've been tracking down the light at the end of the tunnel. I think I've just about found it.

Can I now admit that what happened to me over these past few months had no more to do with God's healing than any run-of-the-mill chemo therapy treatment does? That I was just lucky or resilient? No. I can't. It was just too weird. There were too many strange occurrences and uncommon coincidences. No matter what the outcome now, I cannot say with a pure conscience that I was not touched by God.

I still believe that God is our healer. Having said that, we still have biopsies to accomplish of the affected regions. I am believing that those spots will be found to be benign, or to be gone altogether. But if they're not, I am, once again, going to lean on the example of Hananiah, Mishael and Azariah: I believe that God will save me from this. But even if He doesn't, I will remain firm. God has proven Himself to me more times than I can count. Why would I forsake Him now? If I must travel down this road again, then so be it. There must be more lives for me to touch going that way than going the other. I will not fail. I will stand strong. And I would very much appreciate you standing with me.

There are many things that are different about this time than the last. I'm not going into it flat on my back, for one. But most importantly, I'm not afraid any more. I'm not afraid of this cancer. I'm not afraid of changes to my job or family or life. And that is, for me, a very significant difference.

Disappointment and discouragement can unravel our lives, if we let them. They can poison our souls and leave us only a husk of the person we were supposed to be. But we can choose to rise above them. We can forgive. We can embrace the change. We can fight through and blaze a new trail. We can dare, against all materialistic reason, to hope. And we can find the light.

Who knows: maybe, when we finally reach it, we will find it to be much greater than the light we were originally chasing. Maybe, when all is said and done, we won't see any other way it could have gone.

Until Next Time.
(An Afterword)

"A happy ending is really just the chance for a new beginning."

By this definition, perhaps this is still a happy ending.

This wasn't how the book was supposed to end. In fact, it didn't end this way up until I was days away from finishing it. But, as any writer will tell you, sometimes the story surprises you in the last turn. Just like life.

I wrestled with whether to include all of the content that I did in here. I even struggled a bit on if I should release the book at all. But, in the end, I went with every bit of it. I still believe it to be true, and I still believe all of the messages to be valid. The little blazes of light were enough for me to finish this project and leave it intact. Hopefully you agree.

I don't know what the future holds. I've seen glimpses perhaps, but the coming months are still murky for me. I do not exaggerate when I say that everything in my world is now in flux, with the blessed exception of my family. I have rarely been this unmoored in my life. So why do I feel such peace?

Before I received the impression that the last essay in this book would be on disappointment I seemed to hear God say that he was opening doors that no man could close, and closing doors no man could open. I know that's part of my peace, because that happened before I knew anything was going on. But more than that, I am at peace because I have a good Daddy. My Heavenly Father has never left me. He has never forsaken me. And He's not going to start now.

Maybe you're in a similar place. Maybe the darkness is closing in all around you, and you don't know how to find the light (much less take a breath.) Don't lose hope. Don't lose heart. There is a Champion of Light fighting for you, whether you see him or not.

Why does darkness exist? Why does it so rudely invade our lives? May I put forward the idea that it exists to showcase the light? After all, we would have no idea what light even was if we were not first acquainted with darkness. To paraphrase the movie "Vanilla Sky", how would we know what is sweet if we didn't also know what is sour?

But though we are buffeted on every side, there is still hope. We can make it to daybreak. I truly believe that. For me and for you.

Thank you for reading. I hope that, somehow, this little book has touched you -- whether it's just made you think or shown you another perspective or maybe, just maybe, moved you in some deeper, more wonderful, way. Regardless, I'm grateful you've stuck with it all the way to the end.

But this brings me to a question. If this collection has impacted you, would you do me a favor? Share it with someone who needs it. Pass it on to a friend or a family member or a coworker. And then get involved online at http://www.lifespringseternal.com. Sign up for the email list. Take a look at the prayer page. Let me know what's going on with you. Let's not lose touch.

I thought The Cancer Diaries were finished, but it seems there could very well be a volume two. I look forward to sharing it with you, and all of the miracles it will surely contain, when the time is right.

I pray that you find peace, I pray that you are blessed. And I pray that every day you experience the life-giving wonder of God.

Until next time.

Your Friend,

Byron Leavitt

About Byron

Byron Leavitt lives near Tacoma, Washington in a centennial Swiss-style home surrounded by carnivorous plants and Morning Glory. He is joined by the love of his life, Sarah, their daughters Aurora and Eden, and their stoic butler, Egad. Occasionally people have commented negatively about the dragons, the gargoyle baby, the basement, or even, once in awhile, about Egad himself. Such comments always make Byron smile.

Byron is the author of the novel "Alayaka" (a work in progress that he hopes you will get to read soon) as well as many shorter works of fiction. He is also the writer behind "Life Springs", a place of wonder, darkness and hope. You can learn more about his work on his website, http://www.byronleavitt.com.

When he is not writing in the third person, Byron will often address you as himself. Hi.

Want More Wonder?

Then be sure to go to http://www.lifespringseternal.com where you will find the latest posts, the newest information, and the freshest news from Byron.

While you're there, sign up for the e-mail list to become a part of the Life Springs family and never miss a post again.

What Did You Think?

I would love to hear from you. Drop me a line when you have a minute at byron@byronleavitt.com. Or meet me either on Facebook at http://www.facebook.com/byroncleavitt or on Twitter at http://www.twitter.com/byron_leavitt. God bless you.

References

Dare to Hope

1. Job 13:15
2. Psalms 20:7-8

Beauty in the Rain

3. Daniel 3
4. Image © IStock Photo

Coauthoring Our Destinies

5. Gen. 18:22-33
6. Gen. 4:10
7. Jonah 1:2

There is Peace

8. Matthew 8:23-27; Luke 8:22-25
9. Simon Wiesenthal, "The Sunflower: On the Possibilities and Limits of Forgiveness" (Schocken, 1998).

10. Philippians 4:7

This Island, Man

11. Robert Zemeckis, "Castaway" (Twentieth Century Fox Film Corporation, 2000).

12. Rob Bell, "Drops Like Stars" (Zondervan, 2009).

Our Healer

13. Michael Guglielmucci, "Healer" (Integrity Media, 2008).

14. Mark Batterson, "The Circle Maker" (Zondervan, 2011).

15. Kings 20:1-7

16. Peter 2:24

Life Springs Eternal

17. Psalms 6:5; Psalms 18:5; for more on Sheol, check out the Wikipedia page at http://en.wikipedia.org/wiki/Sheol

18. Ecclesiastes 3:21

19. Ecclesiastes 9:5

20. John 5:29; 1 Corinthians 15:12-21

21. Matthew 22:23; Mark 12:18; Luke 20:27; Acts 23:8; for more on the Sadducees and Pharisees, check out: http://www.catholic.com/quickquestions/please-explain-the-difference-between-the-sadducees-and-the-pharisees-in-the-gospels

22. Randy Alcorn, "Heaven" (Tyndale House Publishers, 2004), 475-482. For more on the Platonic influence

on Christianity, check out: http://geekychristian.com/christianitys-platonic-heaven/

23. Jeffrey Long & Paul Perry, "Evidence of the Afterlife" (HarperOne, 2010). Howard Storm, "My Descent into Death" (Doubleday, 2005). Richard Sigmund, "My Time in Heaven" (Whitaker House, 2010). Mary C. Neal, MD, "To Heaven and Back" (Water Brook Press, 2012). For more on Near Death Experiences, check out http://www.nderf.org.

24. For a thorough examination of the biblical references to Heaven, see Randy Alcorn's book of the same name. (Randy Alcorn, "Heaven" (Tyndale House Publishers, 2004).) I also recommend Dinesh D'Souza's book on the afterlife. (Dinesh D'Souza, "Life After Death: The Evidence" (Regnery Publishing, 2009).)

25. Luke 23:43

26. Corinthians 12:2-3

27. Samuel Stennett, "On Jordan's Stormy Banks I Stand" (1787).

28. 1 Corinthians 15:55b

Where We Go From Here

29. Proverbs 13:12

30. 2 Corinthians 4:1, 6-10, 16-18

Acknowledgments

I always read that it takes a lot of people to write a book.

I don't know about that. I did pretty much this whole thing by myself. The only help I really got was from my wife and a couple semi-critical eyes, as well as some InDesign training videos.

However, I do believe it takes a lot of people to live a life. Especially when you've been living one like I have this past year.

First, thanks to my mother-in-law, Pam, who moved in with us while I was flat on my back and Sarah had her broken toe. We wouldn't have made it through without her. And thanks to my father-in-law, Michael, for giving her up for those months.

Second, thanks to my aunt, Julie, who drove up from Oregon repeatedly to help us and to accompany us to appointments as well as bringing us supplies, remedies, medicine and solutions. She went above and beyond.

Thanks are due also to Mandy, my coworker, who went all kinds of crazy guard dog at work. From putting in air purifiers to hanging up signs that ours was a germ-free office to telling everyone -- including our boss -- that, no, I couldn't be talked to right then no matter how urgent it seemed, she was (and is) awesome.

Thanks to my dad, Chris, and new mom, Marilyn, for always being willing to free up their schedules. Thanks to Peter for understanding my early frustrations with "Invalid Byron." Thanks to Bob and Marissa for dropping everything to drive over monthly from Spokane. Thanks to my mom, Val, my sister, Dawn, and my brothers-in-law Jared and Andrew for their support. Thanks to Pastor Dwain, Pastor Joel, Michael, Harold and the whole office staff for putting up with my absences for doctor's appointments and the occasional weekend, as well as for the prayers.

Speaking of which, thank you to every single person, whether I know you or not, who prayed for me. Your prayers were felt. Your prayers were answered. And they will be again.

Thanks to Eileen, Lauri, Patsy, Dereck, Jack, Barbara, Pastor Gayle and the New Life gang, Kathleen, Teresa and Rick, Steve and Eric. You know what you did (well, at least you probably know what you did.) And it was life-changing.

Thanks to Dr. Chaves, Amy, Debbie, Rita, Deb and the rest of the Northwest Medical Specialties staff. You are all remarkable human beings, and ministering angels for God whether you believe in Him or not. Thanks to all of the chemo patients, too, who let us into their lives - if only for a few hours. May you find healing in the arms of the Healer. (Here's looking at you, Herb and Beth.)

Thanks to everyone who gave to us financially. I honestly don't even know who all of you were. But you do. And I thank you.

Thanks to everyone who gave me encouragement on the blog and let me know how much it was meaning to them. You kept me going. This book wouldn't exist without you.

Thanks to everyone I forgot to mention. Your contribution changed our lives, and just because my memory sucks doesn't mean you aren't valued and cherished.

Almost last but definitely not least, thank you to the most important people in my life, the ones without whom I wouldn't have beaten cancer (or had any reason to): my wife, Sarah (my butterfly), my daughter, Aurora (my princess), my daughter, Eden (my pipsqueak), and my savior, Jesus Christ (my brother and my Lord). I love you all. Once more for the win.

Thank you, God. Your mercies endure forever.

Join the Conversation.

http://www.lifespringseternal.com

http://www.facebook.com/ByronCLeavitt

http://www.twitter.com/Byron_Leavitt

http://www.ByronLeavitt.com

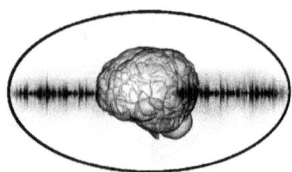

Brain Waves Press

www.ingramcontent.com/pod-product-compliance
Lightning Source LLC
Chambersburg PA
CBHW051957290426
44110CB00015B/2276